STEAM MEMORIES: 1950

No. 21: WEST COAST MAIN LINE
& BRANCHES IN LANCASHIRE

*Including: Wigan, Preston, Lancaster, Morecambe,
Carnforth and Blackpool*

Copyright Book Law Publications 2008
ISBN 1-899624-99-7

INTRODUCTION

County Palatine was indeed blessed with its share of Britain's railway infrastructure. All three of the main constituent companies of the London Midland & Scottish Railway had vast interests there not least the Lancashire & Yorkshire Railway. However, our journey through the county will be taken along the former London & North Western Railway main line, the great Anglo-Scottish trunk route of the West Coast.

This album relies mainly on the photographic exploits of Don Beecroft who made numerous visits to Lancashire in the late 1950s and early 1960s, either by way of family holidays or in following the fortunes of his favourite football team. Contributions from Keith Pirt introduce us to some of the older and less fashionable members of the locomotive world.

Starting in Warrington which, through boundary changes in the early 1970s, nowadays resides in the fair county of Cheshire, we will proceed northwards through Wigan and on to Preston. There we will follow the age old practice of Lancashire folk and take an excursion to the seaside, joined no doubt by others from further afield. Having sampled a couple of the branches and what they had to offer, we resume our trip northwards to Lancaster where we will visit one of the pioneer railway electrification schemes which is now but a memory. Again the seaside is visited by way of the Midland Railway. Later on we skirt the Lancashire coastline where the cream of the WCML locomotive fleet had a chance to show off their prowess before the really hard work started on the gradual climb into the Lake District. Finally we get to Carnforth where one of the lesser constituents of the LMS, the Furness Railway met two of the big boys and managed to establish their own facilities there and which by good fortune are still there today albeit much changed. But then the railway system has changed dramatically in the last forty-odd years since the illustrations in this album were caught on film.. So, enjoy what is essentially a journey up (or is it Down) the WCML through Lancashire in the heady days of BR steam.

David Allen, Newstead, October 2008.

(title page) An early start from platform No.2 at Preston in July 1961. This is the 6.50 a.m. Blackpool—Todmorden starting out from Preston with Stanier Cl.4 tank No.42657 in charge of a hefty nine-coach formation. The arrival time in Todmorden is unknown but the number of stops en route will certainly see this train reaching its destination after 9.00 a.m. no doubt. However, it must have been a useful train for commuters from the west coast into Manchester. The 2-6-4T was, at that time allocated Blackpool Central shed, transferring there from Low Moor in May 1959. Pre-empting the closure of Rigby Road in October 1964, No.42657 re-allocated to Barrow during September but was condemned shortly after arrival for lack of work. In platform No.3 another Stanier tank gets ready for a stop-start commuter job. Just to the left of the 24E engine is Preston No.2A signal box which took care of the through lines on the west side of the station where freights could negotiate the station without hogging platform space. Behind this signal box was the single line Ribble branch to Preston docks. BLP 5398.

Printed and bound by The Amadeus Press, Cleckheaton, West Yorkshire
First published in the United Kingdom by Book Law Publications, 382 Carlton Hill, Nottingham, NG4 1JA

During BR days it could be argued that Warrington had three engine sheds although, in reality, it had two and a stabling point. This is a section of the largest and most important depot of the trio, Dallam which was a former L&NWR shed opened in 1888 as a replacement for an earlier building. Situated north of Bank Quay station on the west side of the WCML, the shed itself covered ten roads and, as can be seen in the illustration, had a northlight roof. The date of this photograph is 14th August 1955 and the roof by then was becoming fairly dilapidated - after 67 years that seems reasonable. The locomotives housed at Dallam in 1955 comprised a mixture of pre-Group designs from not only the L&NWR but also the L&Y and the Midland. LMS standard designs included Fowler and Stanier types covering everything from tank engines to 8F 2-8-0s but nothing much in the way of 'namers' - a real hotchpotch indeed. This is Stanier 2-6-2T No.40202, one of three of the class allocated to Dallam at that time. This engine transferred here from Stoke in July 1953 and left for the former Cheshire Lines shed at Chester Northgate in January 1957. Never popular, wherever they went, the Stanier 3MT was regarded as something of a damp-squid and no improvement on the Fowler 3MT they were built to supplement. The engine shed was rebuilt in 1957 and at the same time the number of covered roads was reduced to nine. *K.R.Pirt 91F.6.*

Our next stop is the two road shed at Arpley, another L&NWR shed but which dated back to 1854 when the Warrington & Altrincham Junction Railway established a running shed on the site. Situated east of and at a lower level to the WCML, the shed housed, especially at weekends, a number of visiting freight locomotives and a couple of Dallam's tank engines engaged on local passenger work. Arpley was a sub-shed of Dallam. Filling the frame here on Sunday 14th August 1955 is Stanier 8F No.48406, a visitor from Heaton Mersey, which is stabled next to one of the three Ivatt Cl.2 tanks allocated to Dallam at this time. Although Arpley was closed in May 1963, whilst Dallam hung on until October 1967, it was the former shed which kept its railway connections because up until recently Arpley was used as a diesel locomotive stabling point whereas Dallam was not so lucky. *K.R.Pirt 91F.5.*

The third and final 'shed' at Warrington was situated at the south side of Central station on the east-west Cheshire Lines main line between Manchester and Liverpool. In August 1955 this location was simply a servicing point for engines 'running round' at Central station and the photograph gives a good impression of the available facilities. A one road through shed had existed here from about August 1873 but had been dismantled by the turn of the century. Originally only one road was available for locomotives but a second road was laid down during WW1 to expand the stabling room and allow a wagon to be brought on site for coaling purposes. J10 No.65166 was from Liverpool's Brunswick engine shed and was having a weekend in Warrington for any number of reasons but most likely it would be there to take an early morning train westwards on the Monday morning. Further down the yard, behind the coal wagon, another J10 hides from the lens of Keith Pirt's camera. *K.R.Pirt 91F.7.*

Putting up a superb smoke screen as it gathers speed along the Down fast on a wet August day in 1967, Britannia No.70023 approaches Wigan (North Western) with a Euston—Perth express which appears to have a couple of former Great Western vehicles at the front of the formation. To the left of the engine, with the municipal gas works as a background, are the former Lancashire & Yorkshire lines which run alongside the WCML for a short distance here before taking an eastward curve towards Ince and then Manchester, whereas in a westerly direction (to the left in the illustration) they drop down into Wallgate station. Note the gradient post showing a gradual east-west three figure ascent followed by a dramatic two digit descent to Wallgate. The inclines here were necessary to lift the L&Y line over Chapel Lane, the River Douglas and the Leeds & Liverpool canal. The adjacent railways found it convenient to put a junction in here which has proved to be useful over the years. *BLP 9338.*

This is BR Standard 9F No.92208 (honestly) at Wigan (North Western) in August 1967 traversing the Up fast line with a long fitted freight. The wet and overcast weather was not the best for photography but enthusiasts knew that as each week went by, on the count-down to August 1968, fewer and fewer steam locomotives remained active. So, it was a matter of urgency - get what you could wherever it was happening - no matter what the weather. Note that the station canopies are bereft of cladding for whatever reason. The station itself had been remodelled in 1941 but twenty-six years later it appears to have less than adequate cover over the platforms. *BLP 9340.*

Viewed from the western end of Wigan (Wallgate) station, Class 5 No.44713 has just passed Wigan No.2 signal box and heads north along the West Coast main line, in August 1967, with a Blackpool bound express from London (Euston). By now of course the locomotives usually associated with such workings, 'Jubilees' and 'Royal Scots' had all been withdrawn so in the absence of diesel motive power and it was left to the Stanier Class 5s to run them to and from Crewe where electric traction took over. Note the number of civil engineering vehicles stabled around this end of the station. In amongst them is a Cravens two-car d.m.u. which has either been made redundant or stabling room for passenger vehicles was at a premium at this time. *BLP 9345.*

Having just departed from Wallgate station, Stanier Cl.5 No.44864 darkens an already murky sky as it sets off for Manchester (Victoria) with the Saturdays only 2.20 p.m. train from Liverpool (Exchange). This photograph was taken from the footbridge which straddled the goods yard on the Up side of North Western passenger station. *BLP 9348.*

Running parallel to the WCML now but still working against the gradient, the 4-6-0 in charge of the Manchester bound train will soon ease off as it tops the rise and starts the downhill run towards Ince. On the left, and in the distance, stand a couple of the numerous goods sheds and warehouses which were dotted around the southern end of North Western station, however, by now these two installations seem somewhat deserted and closure had either taken place or was imminent; that on the left was latterly the Elders Fyffe banana storage where steam heated vans from Liverpool docks were dropped off from trains bound for destinations further inland. The two passenger stations located in this part of Wigan - North Western and Wallgate - were, and still are, doing business in 1967. Both were given the suffix to their original Wigan titles in 1924 once the LMS had taken stock of their new possessions. *BLP 9349.*

The more usual motive power at the head of a Blackpool-Euston train in August 1967. This is English Electric Type 4 D310 whistling away prior to getting the signal to continue its southward journey. In the far distance can be seen Wigan No.1 signal box, of 1941 vintage, seemingly guarding the junction of the Manchester and Crewe lines. The former route can be made out branching off to the left, passing the gas works sidings and the retort house. There was no actual direct connection in the Up direction from the WCML to the Manchester line at this end of the station, but the route could be gained by setting back into either No.1 or No.2 bay platforms. Trains requiring direct connection from the north had to traverse the line through platform No.1 from the north end. *BLP 9351.*

Another southbound express which was diesel hauled was this Glasgow-Euston relief which was not stopping at Wigan. Crewe built and Crewe allocated Brush Type 4 D1633 heads this Up working which four years previously would have had a 'Duchess' in charge. The Brush locomotives would not however reign anywhere near as long on these Anglo-Scottish expresses as the Stanier Pacifics because within three months of this image being captured, the first of the English Electric Co-Co Type 4s (later Class 50) will have been turned out from nearby Vulcan Foundry. By August 1968 that class would have taken over the Anglo-Scottish expresses northwards from Crewe. To accelerate the services prior to electrification, and in the face of stiff competition from the airlines, British Rail double-headed the 2,700 h.p. diesel locomotives on most of the important and heavier trains. Beyond the station nameboards on the right, can be seen another goods yard which had a footbridge built right over its tracks and thence over the line to Wallgate station. *BLP 9352.*

A long way from its glory days on the Western Region, Britannia Pacific No.70022 appears quite neglected at the head of a relief Carlisle-Euston express gliding through Preston station. The TORNADO nameplates have been removed as has the original front numberplate which now has a less than perfect replica in place. The date is August 1967 and the days in the remaining operational life of this engine are fast ticking away. Easily observed are the cut-out hand holds on the smoke deflectors which were only put in after the tragedy involving sister engine No.70026 at Milton near Didcot in November 1955 - the first fatal accident on the Western Region since its formation. Apparently the original hand rails had been a contributory factor into the cause of the accident so the WR 'Brits' all eventually had the rails replaced by the cut-outs. The cool atmosphere of the day emphasises the steam leakage from the 'Brit' which would work as far as Crewe before handing over to more modern motive power. No.70022 was condemned in December 1967 at Kingmoor shed and, after languishing in a goods yard at Carlisle for three months or so, it was hauled, along with No.70014, to the Inverkeithing yard of its new owners, scrap merchant T.W.Ward. The bridge, which was a favourite 'perch' for enthusiasts, connected the station with the Park Hotel, a jointly owned and rather grand establishment run by the Lancashire & Yorkshire and the London & North Western during the heady years of railway travel when alternative fast modes of inland travel did not exist. The hotel is now but a memory, however, it stood proud on its perch overlooking Preston station until steam passed into history too. *BLP 9334.BLP 9333.*

In July 1961 the Blackpool-Euston expresses were still in the hands of 'Jubilees' or 'Royal Scots' from either Blackpool Central or Preston depots. Crewe North and Longsight engines also worked the Flyde coast expresses to and from London. On a rather dull July afternoon in 1961, 5A 'Jubilee' No.45737 ATLAS is seen departing from platform No.6 with a Euston bound express whilst another express - Perth-Euston with BR Standard 8P No.71000 DUKE OF GLOUCESTER in charge - makes its way slowly towards the photographer along the No.8 platform line. On the right are the carriage sidings in the former East Lancashire Railway section of Preston station. Note that the stock is virtually at right angles with the main line. Beyond the end of the row of carriages the train shed of the ELR portion of the station can just be made out, the ELR line having curved very sharply northwards to align with the WCML at that point. The staircase leading to the Park Hotel bridge, from where Don Beecroft took this picture, looking distinctly dilapidated and was hardly a welcoming sight for any prospective customer of the hotel. *BLP 5415.*

'Jubilee' No.45712 VICTORY enters the station in July 1961 with a Derby-Blackpool (Central) excursion. The train will not stop here and by the time it arrives at Blackpool there will probably be a rush for the public conveniences after its passengers had endured a number of hours travelling in the suburban non-corridor sets. Right behind this train came another Blackpool bound excursion with Stanier Cl.5 No.45260 in charge of a similar formation of stock which had originated at Burton-on-Trent. In 1959, Saturday 5th September to be exact, the Lancashire & North West branch of the Railway Correspondence & Travel Society carried out a traffic survey of the trains working to and from the Flyde coast. The reason for the 'day of observations' was carried out because diesel multiple units were fast taking over many of the Blackpool-Manchester services and were also about to do the same on the services to Burnley. To coincide with the end of the summer timetable, it was also the first weekend of the Blackpool Illuminations. So, it was deemed to be a good time to log as many steam hauled through trains as possible. The survey commenced at 7.00 a.m. at Preston and ended there at 8.00 p.m. WCML traffic was not included but during the course of the day 139 coast bound trains were noted, together with numerous light engine movements. In the opposite direction 97 trains and 12 light engine movements were recorded. Further to those trains subject of the survey, another large number travelled outside the qualifying period but between 9.25 p.m. and 1.05 a.m. on the Sunday morning a further 36 return excursion trains left either Central or North stations. The last of these was a nine coach train, including a cafeteria car, headed for Treherbert. It had arrived at Blackpool North at 6.36 a.m. on the Saturday morning so the contingent from South Wales managed breakfast, lunch and dinner in Blackpool during their stay. I wonder how many slept on the way home? *BLP 5413.*

In July 1964 the standard of the external condition of steam motive power was sinking rapidly and Aintree based BR Standard Cl.4 No.75060 was a typical example of the state of cleanliness prevailing at the time. The 4-6-0 is seen at the head of the 2.41 p.m. express to Liverpool (Exchange), a three-coach formation which is starting out from the bay platforms on the ELR side of the station. The curvature of the lines here, compared with the north-south main line, can be gleaned from the main station roof in the background. In the seven years since it came into traffic, No.75060 had covered in excess of 230,000 miles but over the next three years to its withdrawal it would be lucky to reach 300,000 which makes it an expensive vehicle by steam locomotive standards. During its final years of work, the 4-6-0 transferred from Aintree to Edge Hill in June 1965. A year later it was at Heaton Mersey where it was turned around and sent packing to the LMR shed at Chester. They in turn got rid of it a few weeks later to Croes Newydd where, in April 1967 it was condemned. It was purchased by a scrap yard in north-east England for £1,865 which apparently included haulage to the yard in North Blyth. *BLP 6877.*

In charge of a Down parcels train, Crewe North 'Royal Scot' No.46127 OLD CONTEMPTIBLES 1914 AUG.5 to NOV.22, slips through platform No.5 in July 1961. By now this engine had joined the '2 million mile club', the achievement attained at some time during October 1960. Luckily it still had time to notch up more miles when a transfer to Upperby shed in May 1962 gave it a chance of numerous trips, like this, along the WCML before withdrawal took place in the following December. It was cut up at Crewe in May 1963. *BLP 5399.*

Crewe North 'Jubilee' No.45689 AJAX rests in platform No.6 after its arrival with a Barrow—Preston express in July 1961. This engine spent twenty-three years of its life working from 5A. After starting work from Crewe when new in February 1936, it ended its days there in December 1964. Other sheds which saw its services for various periods of time included Longsight, Bushbury, Edge Hill, Llandudno Junction and Trafford Park. On the right is BR Standard Cl.2 No.78037, one of the Preston pilots which was resting with a rake of coaches in the dead-end road which lay end-on to the ELR carriage sidings. Just over twelve months previously, the six year old 2-6-0 was damaged, along with numerous other locomotives, during a serious fire at Preston shed but after the relevant repairs were carried out on the locomotive it was released back to traffic and does not appear to have suffered unduly. By now it was using Lostock Hall shed as home, although still on the books at Preston. When Preston shed was closed for operational purposes in September 1961, the Cl.2 was sent off to Skipton for further service. *BLP 5401.*

Class leader No.46220 CORONATION reverses onto a Down empty milk train waiting in platform No.5 in July 1961. Already the growing fleet of English Electric Type 4 diesel-electrics has relegated a number of these superb engines onto duties such as this. The 'Duchess' will work this particular train as far as Carlisle where the various vans and tanks will be split and returned to dairies all over the area to be washed out, refilled with milk and got ready for the following day's Up train. The process was continuos and required another set of vehicles to balance the Up and Down perishables workings. Although No.46220 started and finished its life allocated to sheds in England, it did spend almost twenty years working from Polmadie shed from December 1939 to July 1958. Withdrawn in April 1963, it did not fulfil its 'laid down' economic life of thirty years and was short by about three years. However, that did not reflect on the design or indeed the performance of the class, its was all down to the dieselisation of the WCML and the march of progress. *BLP 5404.*

In glorious mid morning sun light (it was July 1961), one of the unnamed 'Patriots' No.45542 leaves platform No.1 with a train for Manchester (Victoria). The palatial building in the right background, situated on Fishergate, is the County Hall, which was to move a short distance to modern, less elaborate premises within a few years of this picture being taken. The unnamed 'Pat' had been a resident of Preston shed since November 1958, after many years at Upperby, and managed to survive the disastrous fire which destroyed the roof of Preston engine shed on Tuesday 28th June 1960. Ordered pre-Stanier, the 4-6-0 was built just three years before the 'Duchess' which featured in the last illustration but it was to be withdrawn eleven months after this particular working took place. *BLP 5406.*

Using the avoiding lines which skirted the western edge of the station, adjacent to platform No.1, Stanier Cl.5 No.45303 heads south with a lengthy Up freight. To the left is the goods warehouse situated near to and known as Christian Road. This picture precedes a bridge which straddled the warehouse and linked a new Post Office sorting centre built on its west side, with the railway facility between platforms No.5 and 6. *BLP 5410.*

21

The morning Manchester (Victoria)—Glasgow (Central) express, with Carnforth based unnamed Patriot No.45513 in charge, waits for the signal to proceed beneath Fishergate bridge and on to the north in July 1961. Some of the lighter weight Manchester—Glasgow trains were combined at Preston with similar trains from Liverpool and these usually required more substantial motive power than was on offer here such as a 'Britannia', 'Clan' or occasionally a 'Princess' or a 'Duchess'. However, whenever a through train was timetabled, 'Patriots' of both denominations were used, along with 'Jubilees', 'Scots', 'Brits' and even Class 5s. Note a Blackpool bound excursion has taken to the Down slow line with a train made up of Gresley stock. *BLP 5425.*

Another 'Duchess' why not!. This is No.46227 DUCHESS OF DEVONSHIRE also heading for Glasgow and right behind the 'Patriot' with an express from Birmingham in the summer of 1961. With plenty of steam available, the Pacific looks every bit the part of graceful power and strength. One of the Polmadie based members of the class, it was amongst the first casualties being written off in December 1962; still in good nick and with plenty of life in it but nevertheless surplus to requirements. *BLP 5428*.

We go forward in time now to the period when the remaining Stanier Pacifics were about to give in and call it a day. Hardly taking their place but nonetheless working some of the lesser traffic handled by the 'Duchesses', the 'Brits' became regular performers on the WCML until their general demise too, in 1967. This in No.70043 **LORD KITCHENER**, complete with all the necessary plates, heading a Carlisle bound parcels train past Preston No.5 signal box in July 1964. The photographer is standing in the middle of the Blackpool roads (yes he did have the necessary permits) and has taken advantage of a lull in traffic. To the left of the 'Brit' is the Maudlands goods yard. To the right and just out of sight is the damaged and by now long closed Preston engine shed. *BLP 6875.*

In its heyday, Preston shed had a number of Stanier 'Jubilees' allocated and this is No.45633 ADEN on the afternoon of Monday 14th April 1958. Having just been topped-up at the coaling plant, the 4-6-0 is blowing off with a nice head of steam, ready to head a southbound working. The servicing facilities at Preston motive power depot were situated on the western side of the shed, so that a frustrating glimpse was all you got from a passing train. *K.R.Pirt 217.5.*

Inside the roofless and derelict engine shed in July 1964 with condemned 'Royal Scot' No.46168 THE GIRL GUIDE stored and awaiting its fate. Withdrawn week ending 2nd May last, the 4-6-0 was hauled from its then home shed at Springs Branch to Preston shed. Shortly after this scene was captured on film, No.46168 was taken to Crewe works and broken up. Note that all the necessary plates are still in place; obviously Preston was regarded as a 'secure' storage facility. Many other engines were kept here after their withdrawal and amongst the notables were a dozen unrebuilt Patriots, a couple of Jubilees and the BR built Duchess, No.46257 CITY OF SALFORD albeit without its nameplates. *BLP 6876.*

Before we gallivant off to the seaside, a visit to Blackburn would not go amiss. Here at Lower Darwen engine shed we find Lanky 'A' class No.52526 on the turntable which was situated at the north end of the shed yard. The date is 19th September 1955, and the grass has attained its luxuriant growth and appears to be ready for burning off during the 'dry spell'. The stone bridge parapet in the right background carried a path across the railway line which was at a lower elevation to this part of the shed yard. Off to the left was Ewood Park, the home of Blackburn Rovers and within shouting distance from this point. If this was a Saturday afternoon (its actually a Monday) and the Rovers were at home the engine would be 'stuck' on the turntable all afternoon for some reason and with shed staff perched on the boiler, cab roof, etc. - goodness knows why. Note the lamp by the firebox which was hooked onto an iron fitted specifically for the purpose of storing the item out of the way but at the same time making it easily accessible. The 0-6-0 was a resident of this shed until March 1957 when it transferred 'up the road' to Rose Grove. In October 1959 Lostock Hall had it for six months before it travelled back inland to Bury. Note how most of these exL&Y engines stuck to familiar sheds. Withdrawn in March 1961, the Horwich built engine was just fifty-two years old. *K.R.Pirt 22H.8.4.* 27

Sunday 6th September 1959 - Blackpool Central engine shed (aka Rigby Road) . This was not just any old Sunday morning, this was the holiday period in Blackpool when train after train arrived from virtually all over the country. Blackpool's Central and North stations took the influx in their stride whilst South station took care of a few too. The shed yard is slowly filling up but already resident are a couple of Rebuilt Patriots No.45526 MORECAMBE AND HEYSHAM on the right, with No.45530 SIR FRANK REE dominating the picture and sandwiched between BR Standard Cl.4 tank No.80046 and 'Crab' No.42829. This is the morning line-up with everything facing south and ready for the afternoon and evening departures. In the meantime the shed will slowly fill so that every road will be brimming with visiting engines. Many of these will be shunted further into the shed but that job took some organising so that engines could be released at specific times without delay. Patriot No.45526, a Carlisle Upperby engine, had come in the night before after working into Central station with the 1.30 p.m. express from Euston (W93) which arrived one minute late at 7.23 p.m. The chalked-on reporting number still adorns the smokebox. Also ex London during the previous evening, the other 'Pat' was a Longsight engine which brought an earlier express, the 10.45 a.m. ex Euston (W77), into Central some twenty minutes late at 5.10 p.m. It also still sports the reporting number. Another Longsight engine on shed at this time was 'Scot' No.46131 THE ROYAL WARWICKSHIRE REGIMENT which had reporting number W130. The Standard tank was part of the 24E allocation and had arrived here in November 1957 but this would be its last season at Blackpool because it transferred to Glasgow's Corkerhill shed in May 1960. *BLP 2778.*

This is 'Crab' No.42829, which apparently had brought a very early morning excursion in from Burton-on-Trent and was now being used by the disposal gang to shunt the shed yard. Note it is one of the five Horwich moguls fitted with rotary cam poppet valve gear, a fitting which was to cause their early demise compared with the rest of the class. All five of the poppet valve engines were allocated to Burton at this time and any one of them could turn up at Blackpool as the resort was a popular destination for the good people of Burton wanting some time at the seaside. Of course September was the start of the Illuminations season at Blackpool and day-trippers would stream into the town in their tens of thousands every day, more so at weekends, and the railway managed to cope everyday. *BLP 2780.*

29

Hauling a train of empty stock into Spen Dyke carriage sidings is Stanier Cl.3 No.40091, one of the Central pilots on this Sunday 6th September 1959. Note the twinned adornment but crudely painted 24E shed code applied to the smokebox door. The 2-6-2T had only just transferred to Blackpool during the previous August from Shrewsbury so that explains the absence of a cast shed plate, although one would have thought that the shed stores might have had one in stock. The continuous movement of empty stock was a big challenge at Blackpool but with decades of experience the shunters, pilots and signalmen rarely had a problem and if one arose they were quick to put it right before they ran out of time. 24E proved to be the last posting for this well travelled engine and withdrawal took place in October 1961. It was sold for scrap to the Central Wagon Co. and cut up at their Ince yard. *BLP 2776.*

Now here is an early start for homeward bound holidaymakers in October 1964. The train is a Manchester relief and it is hauled by Cl.5 No.45003. We are virtually midway between Central and South stations, looking north-east from Bloomfield Road bridge. The train is passing the Spen Dyke carriage sidings which appear to be fairly depleted of stock at this time of the year but, something sinister was afoot concerning these carriage sidings, the engine shed and indeed the whole stretch of railway from South station to the terminus at Central. Spen Dyke sidings consisted fourteen roads but just to the south of this location were two more carriage yards - Bloomfield Road also of fourteen roads and, to the east of that fan, Waterloo Road which had a further twelve sidings. Central (Rigby Road) engine shed is hidden by the exhaust from the Cl.5. In its railway heyday, the Blackpool yards could not always cope with the amount of empty stock which required storage, prior to returning home, so they would send the overflow to Fleetwood and then to stations all the way down the lines on the two separate routes to Kirkham North. Further afield, Lostock Hall and Horwich were also used, the latter place being used on Saturday 5th September 1959 for the final time. Note the stands and floodlight tower of Blackpool FC beyond the carriages. This whole stretch of railway property, from South station to the throat of Central is now one huge parking lot where day-trippers can leave their motor vehicles and take a short walk to the promenade and the delights of Blackpool. *BLP 7236.*

31

The throat of Blackpool (Central) station in October 1964 with old and new(ish) motive power, side by side. On the right, at platform No.9 and looking rather immaculate for the period, is Low Moor based 'Jubilee' No.45565 VICTORIA with a return excursion for Bradford (Exchange) - 1N78. Surprisingly the 4-6-0 was not ex works and the highly polished finish is all down to the cleaners at 56F. Those of you with eagle eyes will have noted that the fireman, leaning against the bridge parapet and looking down into Chapel Street, has bulled-up his boots so that their shine matches that of the locomotive - there was still some pride and respect for the job back then, even if the higher echelons did not promote it. On the left, alongside platform No.7, stands Brush Type 2 diesel D5849 which is heading train 1X08, another return excursion which is bound for Sheffield (Midland). This part of the station constitutes the uncovered excursion platforms which would be deserted during the winter period, whereas in the summer they became extremely busy, especially during the morning and evening. The main station at Central stood to the left and was a typical medium size terminus station able to cope with normal timetabled traffic and the long distance trains. This illustration was one of the final photographs showing the excursion platforms in use because on Monday 2nd November the whole station was closed, traffic being diverted to North station at Talbot Road. A great tradition had come to an abrupt end. The motor vehicle had won but at least this station managed to reach a grand old age of 101 years. *BLP 7246.*

Back at Central shed in October 1964 the atmosphere was a little less hectic than in previous years and this Bank Hall 'Jubilee' finds itself virtually alone during its afternoon break. No.45627 SIERRA LEONE had spent most of its life working on the old Midland Division of the LMS and the BR counterpart. After ending up at Canklow in December 1961, with the closure of Millhouses shed, it seems that its life was rapidly coming to an end but a transfer to Bank Hall three months later gave it a new lease and the 4-6-0 remained operational until September 1966 by which time less than a dozen of the class remained active. Note the numerous, probably hundreds out of picture, of motor coaches in the yard on the right. At Blackpool Illuminations time, day trips by charabang became the norm - virtually door-to-door cheap travel - and hundreds, if not thousands, of these private coaches would descend on the resort weekends. During the week the coaches tended to bring people in the evening for a slow drive along the promenade and then set off to a pub for a couple of drinks before heading home. The railways found it more and more difficult to win back passenger traffic from the coach firms and the decline became more rapid as the 60's decade was entered and private motoring became ever more popular. One can imagine that the crew of No.45627 were possibly partaking some form of liquid refreshment during their extended stay at Blackpool - a perk that most crews relished on the longer stay overs. *BLP 7260.*

In October 1961 Blackpool Central had this Preston based 'Royal Scot' on shed. A regular visitor, it was however soon to move on. After a colourful and interesting thirty-four years plodding the tracks of the west coast main line, No.46165 THE RANGER 12th LONDON REGT. ended its days at Annesley shed in Nottinghamshire, working the Marylebone expresses and semi-fasts from Nottingham (Victoria) through the spring and summer of 1964. By then, it had probably notched up about 1,900,000 miles and according to the Annesley footplate staff, '...you could tell!' It was one of the shortest lived Annesley 'Scot' allocations recorded. Re-allocated back to WCML metals at Crewe North shed in November 1964, the 4-6-0 never actually got there because it was condemned at Annesley on the very day it was due to transfer westwards. No.46165 was later sold for scrap to a large concern situated just east of Sheffield. They cut it up in early 1965. Rigby Road engine shed roof had been rebuilt in 1958 using a lightweight steel frame structure clad in corrugated asbestos but the depot was not offered any modern means to service its own and visiting locomotives. The original Lancashire & Yorkshire coaling stage with its water tank over, seen on the left of the picture, sufficed to the closure of the depot. Ash handling also relied, as it had done since the earliest days, on man power. Remarkably the hard standing outside the shed is virtually free of ash and clinker unlike many other sheds at this time when piles of the stuff littered the ground. *BLP 5724.*

Blackpool (North) station was less than a mile from Central - as the seagull flies - but by rail the mileage got into double figures so that locomotive servicing required a shed dedicated to such at the North site. Much smaller than Central's Rigby Road shed, the North shed at Talbot Road comprised just three roads offering cover for the local engines out-shedded from Central shed. Visiting engines, such as BR Standard 9F 2-10-0 No.92132, made do with the yard facilities which were adequate although mechanical coaling was never introduced at either this shed or its parent and much busier establishment at Central. The date is 6th September 1959 and the Leicester Midland based 9F had brought an excursion, reporting number M9, from Leicester (London Road) on the day before, arriving at Blackpool (North) with the nine-coach coach formation at 2.21 p.m., some twelve minutes early on the schedule. It had departed from Leicester at 9.50 a.m. but its route is unknown. most probably it was Midland main line, Hope valley, Manchester Victoria, then via Preston. When the 9F worked back to Leicester is unknown but possibly a Sunday evening return excursion was its most likely way. It was not the only 9F to visit Blackpool that weekend as another Leicester based engine, No.92019 arrived at North station on the Saturday morning with M17, a nine-coach excursion from Sheffield (Midland), also via the Hope valley line. Then, at 3.01 p.m. on Saturday afternoon, Saltley based No.92137 ran into Central with a ten-coach excursion No.977 which had originated at Heeley. No.92019 departed less than three hours later with M17, the 2.20 p.m. North to Sheffield (Midland) duty consisting the same nine vehicles which it brought into Blackpool. Note the sun - proof that it was not always raining here. *BLP 2783.*

Caprotti Class 5 No.44744 of Longsight had also worked into Blackpool (North) on the Saturday with the late running - 30 minutes - 9.40 a.m. Stoke-on-Trent to Blackpool (N) reporting No.W123. The ten-coach train made up the 1.55 p.m. return working less than two hours after its arrival in Blackpool but whereas the stock was utilised further that day, the 9A Caprotti 4-6-0 was put onto the shed for servicing before working back to Manchester on an unknown duty. The lighting towers were erected during the rebuilding phase of this shed in 1957 and added much needed illumination to the shed yard during the long winter months especially. *BLP 2785*.

Fleetwood is at the end of another of the branches radiating from the WCML. Renowned once for its for its fishing fleet, Isle of Man ferries, terminus for Blackpool trams and not much else, the town was something of a backwater and the railway tended to treat it as such, even in the heyday of the Flyde coast holiday resorts. Its only boat train originated in Manchester and intending passengers from elsewhere in the country had to board that at Preston. Fore the railway enthusiast the place did not have much to offer either. Namers consisted the occasional 'Jubilee' heading the above named train but that motive power was usually a Stanier Class 5 but Lanky 'A' class 0-6-0s have been known to haul those trains too. However, there were a couple of gems which resided at Fleetwood shed and which worked exclusively within the town boundary so, if you wanted to 'cop' them it meant a trip to the seaside or, if you were lucky, you saw them on a visit to Horwich works perhaps when they went for overhauls. Ex LMS dock tank No.47161 was one such engine and is seen shunting the dock side sidings in May 1949. The short wheelbase 0-6-0T was one of a pair, the other was No.47165, which served at 24F, or 28B to give the shed its early BR coding, for much of the BR period. Three more of the class worked from Birkenhead or Bidston sheds on the Wirral whilst the remaining five members of the class were resident in Scotland. So, other than these two, a handful of the ubiquitous Cl.5s, 'Crabs' and the mundane 2-6-4T, with perhaps a super WD 2-8-0 thrown in, that is all Fleetwood had to offer the trainspotter. *BLP 3771.* 37

How about this for a trip working? exLMS 3F 0-6-0T No.47599, with steam to spare, works a long train of mainly loaded container flats under the wires on the Midland line from Lancaster Green Ayre to Heysham in July 1963. The train has just left Lancaster and is approaching the Carlisle bridge which carries the WCML over the River Lune and the Midland route. Don Beecroft, who is getting a wave from the driver, took the photograph from the pedestrian footpath which is attached to the east side of the bridge. The bridge itself was being rebuilt and after a year long renewal which, at certain times, saw WCML trains diverted over this old MR route, scaffolding still encased the spans whilst the concrete parapets had yet to be fixed. No doubt more weekend possessions would be required before completion. The north bank of the River Lune, with its mud flats and grass banking, can be seen on the right, whilst over to the left was the A589, the road which linked Morecambe with the old A6 and the outside world. The 3F tank and its train is bound for the docks at Heysham where the containers will be loaded onto one of the ships plying trade across the Irish Sea to Belfast. Note that three continental ferry vehicles are slotted into the middle of the formation. *BLP 6287.*

A little later Stanier 2-6-4T No.42464 hurries away from Lancaster (Green Ayre) station with a Skipton—Morecambe train. The load is hardly taxing for the Cl.4 tank so some brisk running would have been in order over numerous stretches of the line from Skipton. All of the route over which this train traversed, after leaving the Midland main line at Wennington, and including this section from Lancaster to Morecambe, has now gone. Carnforth shed supplied the engine for this particular working and for other cross Pennine trains too such as the Morecambe—Leeds passenger services, however, No.42464 would soon move on to Blackpool for different duties prior to ending its days at Newton Heath in 1965. *BLP 6289*.

The aforementioned Carlisle bridge with two trains crossing and both working tender first. Coming from the south is 'Jubilee' No.45655 KEITH whilst the Stanier Class 5 working south is unidentified on account of the filth obscuring its number. This is the western face of the bridge as seen from the embankment above the A589 road. The electrified Midland line is just out of view below the cast iron railings, although part of the catenary is visible. Apparently, part of the bridge rebuilding entailed the strengthening of the piers besides renewing the spans. Hopefully that work will give the bridge a further 150 years of life. *BLP 6285.*

A more dramatic view of the bridge with a Manchester—Morecambe train crossing in July 1963. The motive power is (appropriately nicknamed) Black 5 No.45126 which although in a terrible external condition was in fine fettle and would keep going for another four years. From this angle it is easy to appreciate the size of the piers compared with the train overhead. Even the approach viaduct o the south bank of the Lune is a substantial structure. Note the various signals clinging to the viaduct. The overhead catenary spanning the Lancaster—Morecambe line at this spot and westwards towards Scale Hall station, was installed to test certain structures which would eventually be used on the Manchester—London and WCML electrification scheme; this particular section was built to simulate tunnel clearances. Even then, in 1963, with closure imminent, this pioneering railway was being usefully employed for research and development of future projects. BLP 6288.   41

Remember these, the ex LMS 2P 0-4-4T? They do at Lancaster Green Ayre shed. By the summer of 1951 half of the class were resident at Green Ayre - engine Nos.41900 to 41904 to be exact - for a specific reason. The class was not one of the most popular produced by the LMS and although everybody tried to make the best of them, they continued to perform less than satisfactorily. This engine arrived at Lancaster in July 1950 from Gloucester Barnwood and went into storage almost immediately until February 1951 when it was teased into working a newly introduced push-pull service over the former electrified lines from Lancaster to Morecambe and Heysham. That particular work lasted until August 1953 when the electric railway started up again. In this 28th August 1955 view it has obviously undertaken some recent work but is probably laid up for the weekend (it was a Sunday). In June 1956 Lancaster managed to get rid of the 0-4-4T to Longsight and they in turn sent it back to Gloucester after it spent virtually the whole of its twelve months at 9A in store. The other members of the class which darkened the doors of Green Ayre arrived at varying times: No.41901 came from Manningham in June 1946 and after eight years moved on to Crewe North of all places. No.41902 came to 11E from Bristol in July 1950, probably coupled to 41900, and it too was put into storage until the following February when it started work on the push-pull trains but in March 1954, not required anymore, it transferred to Walsall. Lancaster got No.41903 from Derby in February 1951 and although it went to Rugby in October 1955, it returned to Lancaster during March 1956. No.41904 was another refugee from Bristol no doubt arriving with 41900 and 41902. No.41904 proved to be the longest residing member of the class at Lancaster putting just over nine years in at the former Midland shed, many of those in store. All of the class except No.41900 were condemned in November 1959 and sent for scrap. The survivor was sent on various jaunts to try it out on passenger workings but it never seemed to make any friends. After being in store at the ex GWR shed at Wellington, Shropshire from some time in 1960 until February 1962, it was transferred to Leamington in March 1962 but never got there and instead it went for scrapping at Crewe works. What endings for the others? Nos.41903 and 41904 ended up at the Barrow yard of the Central Wagon Co. No.41901 was cut up at Statford works having spent its remaining years at Watford Junction shed. No.41902 was sold to Cashmores at Great Bridge. *K.R.Pirt 96F.4.*

Lancaster Green Ayre shed was home to a number of the ex LMS Compounds virtually right up to the time when the class was made extinct in 1961. By mid-summer 1935 two of the class - Nos.929 and 930 - were resident although nearby Carnforth had eleven, a mixture of Midland and LMS types (the importance of Carnforth to the MR was a throwback to the days when they used the Furness Railway port at Barrow for their Irish traffic prior to the creation of Heysham as their own port in 1904). No.41065 was one of the Derby built lot from 1925 which started life at Kingmoor but eventually ended up at Green Ayre before Nationalisation. When BR came into being eight Compounds were resident, some being former residents of the closed MR shed at Carnforth. Again the mixture was MR and LMS. By 28th August 1955, when this picture was taken, all of the MR built engines had gone for scrap but nine examples of the post-Grouping engines hung on at Lancaster - Nos.41045, 41065, 41081, 41107, 41108, 41136, 41152, 41196 and 41197. Their work entailed running the passenger services to Leeds, Morecambe and Heysham, keeping within the old boundaries of the Midland for most of the time. No.41065 was condemned in March 1956 but others came to Green Ayre shed to replace it and other withdrawn 4Ps. *K.R.Pirt 96F.5.*

No longer a Compound job in July 1963, the 4.20 p.m. Morecambe (Promenade)—Leeds (City) departs from Lancaster (Green Ayre) station with Stanier Cl.5 No.45196 in charge. The first station at Green Ayre was opened by the Midland Railway in 1848 but the stone built structure in frame dates from about 1870. Closure of this station took place from 3rd January 1966 and eventually the railway itself was to disappear, the final section lasting until 1976 when the demolition of Green Ayre station took place also. The 1966 closure saw one of the country's pioneer overhead electrification schemes - the Lancaster, Morecambe & Heysham 6,600 volts overhead system - relegated to history. The electric railway opened in 1908 and linked Heysham with Morecambe, then Morecambe to Lancaster Green Ayre, then finally Green Ayre to the LNWR station at Lancaster Castle. The rolling stock used on the railway finally gave out in 1951 and the steam powered push-pull service was introduced until August 1953 when 'new' rolling stock in the shape of three surplus 1914 vintage former LNWR 3-car sets from the Willesden Junction—Earls Court line. A fourth set arrived in 1957 but Beeching regarded the whole electrified railway in the area as a loss maker, the result being total closure in January 1966. The train is approaching Skerton bridge which was the eastern limit of the overhead catenary; the sub station which fed the wires was sited on the other side of the line near the goods yard. No.45196 transferred from Crewe North to Green Ayre in March 1963 but the 4-6-0 was reallocated to Rose Grove in October 1964 wherein it nearly made it to the end of BR steam but not quite as it was condemned in December 1967. *BLP 6290.*

Stanier Cl.5 No.44904 speeds through Scale Hall with a Morecambe (Promenade)—Leeds (City) express in July 1963. Note that the station is built to the style which BR went on to use on all their rebuilding on the Manchester—Crewe line and on hundreds of other stations throughout the system using modern, simplistic and clean lines with no elaborate ornamentation. So, was Scale Hall a pioneer for future wayside station design? It appears so. What is certain about this place was its somewhat short operational life. Opened on the 8th June 1957, as the only intermediate station between Lancaster and Morecambe, it closed with the rest of the electric railway on 3rd January 1966. Apparently it virtually paid for itself in three and a half years but that did not impress the short sighted accountants who held the menacing axe. *BLP 6283*.

'Royal Scot' No.46144 HONOURABLE ARTILLERY COMPANY enters platform No.3 at Lancaster (Castle) station in July 1963 with the Down LAKES EXPRESS. We are looking south from the Up No.4 platform. On the extreme left are platforms Nos.5 and 6 which served the electrified line from Lancaster (Green Ayre) station - the Castle branch. The 'Scot' had recently transferred to Crewe North from Llandudno Junction and this was to be its last summer of work before withdrawal. Already the engine had clocked up more than two million miles of revenue earning service and even at its frequency of overhauls its was getting worn out. *BLP 6292.*

This end of the Down platform at Castle station was a regular haunt for trainspotters and you can see why. With the signal set for a clear road, the driver of No.46144 looks back for the green flag before opening the regulator. Note that although the first coach, M6851M is not a new vehicle, it has recently had a thorough overhaul and looks good with a freshly applied coat or two of paint and lining. *BLP 6293*.

The north end junction at Lancaster (Castle) where the line to Glasson dock turns away to the left at the end of platform No.3. Just behind the photographer, and to the left, were bay platforms Nos.1 and 2, the former served the erstwhile Glasson dock branch passenger trains which ceased in July 1930 after forty-seven years service. Latterly in had been used by the Morecambe local trains. No.2 bay platform held stopping trains to Barrow and the Cumbrian coast, besides the local trains to Morecambe (Euston Road) also. The large signal box, Lancaster No.4, had 144 levers and, as can be seen, commanded an excellent view of all it controlled. Coasting in from the north, a rather filthy Class 5, No.45014 of Lancaster Green Ayre, has charge of a Barrow to Preston train and is stopping at the station. The 'Black' 5 spent its first twelve years of life working from Inverness shed but ended up in England by the time BR came into existence. It had moved to Green Ayre in June 1962 from Carnforth and would return there in April 1966 when Green Ayre shed was closed. On the extreme right is the Castle branch to Green Ayre which remained open some ten years after the electric services finished to allow coal trains to service Lancaster's power station. Both of these branch lines, like the 4-6-0, are now history. *BLP 6295.*

A rather pleasant shot of Lancaster (Castle) station in July 1963 with a Manchester—Windermere service setting off from platform No.3 with Cl.5 No.44947 in charge of the lightweight load. This relatively young engine spent the whole of its operational life in Lancashire, starting in February 1946 at Rose Grove then moving on to Blackpool the following June. Except for a one month loan to Accrington in January 1952, the 4-6-0 was at Blackpool until Rigby Road shed closed in September 1964. Then it was off to Bolton until withdrawal in June 1968. Horwich built the engine but it was, alas, scrapped in Kettering unable to complete something most Lancastrians managed to achieve. On the left can be seen the lattice style catenary masts of the Lancaster, Morecambe & Heysham electrification. These dated from the opening of the line and were unusual for the period, or at least on the Midland, because most of the catenary throughout the rest of the line consisted mainly of wooden poles. The London & North Western Railway insisted that lattice steel girders be used if the MR service was to use their station and run alongside their main line, and so these were duly erected in 1908. Although double track at this point, the electrified line becomes single once it veers away from the WCML. For the route down to Green Ayre, the MR introduced what is thought to be the first use of tokenless block signalling in the United Kingdom. Once again, the eagle eyed amongst you will probably have spotted the Metrovick Co-Bo diesel which has just arrived in bay platform No.2 with a service from Barrow; neither its number nor its presence seem to have been acknowledged by Don Beecroft and its inclusion on this picture appears to have been purely accidental. *BLP 6297.* 49

Castle station, July 1963. Coming to a stand at platform No.3, with a Crewe—Workington relief (1L16 ?), is Upperby based Stanier 'Duchess' No.46225 DUCHESS OF GLOUCESTER. Looking fairly clean, the big engine was to become the longest lived (in operational terms) member of the class putting in twenty-five years and seven months service. Only three others got near that total:- Nos.46222 and 46223 with twenty-five years and six months, and No.46224 with twenty-five years and five months. No.46225 also comes out on top with revenue earning mileage too with 1,725,116 miles under its belt. The nearest rival for that accolade was literally miles away with No.46240 notching up a creditable 1,685,042 miles. Although the Pacific was allocated at one time or another to each of the main 'Duchess' depots - Camden, Crewe North, Polmadie and Upperby - it spent very little time at the Glasgow shed in comparison to the others. Therefore, its mileage figures might have had a helping hand because the Scottish based Pacifics averaged approximately 55,000 miles a year as against 60,000 plus miles for the England based engines. However, from January to June 1955 No.46225 was allocated to the Rugby testing station and revenue miles would not have been possible during that period. But, for all the superlative figures and achievements, the big engine was still hauled away for scrap after its withdrawal at Upperby shed on Saturday 12th September 1964. *BLP 6261.*

There was only one intermediate station on the L&NWR's Morecambe branch and that was at Bare Lane, a rather handsome station dating from 1864. Arriving at the Up platform in July 1963 was Ivatt Cl.4 No.43124 with a Morecambe (Euston Road)—Lancaster (Castle) service. The original signal box was situated on the Down platform behind the photographer but the LMS built the present cabin next to the level crossing for obvious reasons. When the station was completed in August 1864 it carried the name Poulton-Le-sands for a short while but this changed to Bare Lane before the end of the year. The double track route from the WCML came in from Hest Bank in the north but was later singled because the anticipated export goods traffic did not materialise. However, in 1888 a double track branch was laid to give access to the WCML from the south, at Morecambe South Junction, and a direct route to Lancaster (Castle) was achieved. With the line from Bare Lane to Morecambe by now singled, it was not until 1891 that a second line was relaid but the branch to Hest Bank remained single. Although temporarily closed for five months in 1994, in connection with the upgrading of the Morecambe branch, Bare Lane station remains open to this day. *BLP 6244.*

In glorious summer sunshine the 10.41 a.m. Morecambe (Euston Road) to Lancaster (Castle) rumbles over the crossing into Bare Lane station in July 1963 with 'Crab' No.42776 in charge. The motive power used on these local trains was varied to say the least. Other classes noted during the same period included Ivatt Cl.2 2-6-2T, Fowler Cl.4 2-6-4T, Stanier Cl.4 2-6-4T, Rebuilt 'Patriot' (No.45535 in July 1963), 'Jubilee' (No.45741 also in July 1963). Strangely Stanier Cl.5s were noticeable by their absence. *BLP 6260.*

After a spell at Crewe works receiving its last overhaul, Holbeck 'Jubilee' No.45675 HARDY gallops past the carriage sidings to the west of Bare Lane with a Crewe—Morecambe (Promenade) service in July 1964. Seen from Broadway bridge, the train will soon start to slow for the junction with the Green Ayre line beyond Euston Road. Virtually deserted, the carriage sidings are a left-over from the days (not so long back) when empty stock from excursion traffic to Euston Road and Promenade stations stabled here to await the return workings. It seems somewhat ironic that the route to Morecambe created by the Midland Railway no longer exists whilst their terminal station (Promenade) survives to serve the resort. On the other hand the route laid down by the L&NWR survives intact as the only railway linking the town, and Heysham, with the rest of the network but their terminal station (Euston Road) was closed from the time of the last train leaving on Saturday 7th September 1963. Euston Road had in fact, since 15th September 1958, been closed during the winter months and only opened to handle summer traffic. Another irony, perhaps, is that when the LNW first reached Morecambe in August 1864 they used the MR station until their own permanent terminus at Euston road was completed in May 1886. No.45675 was most probably on a running-in turn from Crewe or was making its way home to Leeds by various routes but which ever way it went, it managed to survive until June 1967 and was one of the last operational members of the class. Unusual amongst the 'Jubilees' it only ever had two homes - Upperby from December 1935 and Holbeck from October 1948. *BLP 6808.*

The view westwards from Broadway bridge near Bare Lane shows the independent carriage line from Euston Road (that station was situated just beyond the bridge in the distance) running alongside the main line. Approaching on this damp July day in 1964 is Green Ayre based Ivatt Cl.2 No.46422 with a Morecambe—Lancaster (Castle) local service made up of three passenger vehicles and two parcels vans. *BLP 6809.*

The south side of Morecambe (Promenade) station in July 1963 with LMS Ivatt Cl.2 No.41215 heading a local service on platform No.4. Stabled is one of the three-car electric units with Driving Trailer Open Second M29023M leading and ready, according to the destination blind, for a Heysham service. Within thirty months the electric railway will cease to exist and the ancient stock will have gone for scrap. That only four three-car units worked the services and with one of them as spare or in under overhaul, their working must have been fairly intense at times. The fact that they had to reverse at Morecambe to gain the Heysham branch after arrival from Lancaster, and vice versa, did not speed up the service. Albeit the distances involved were not great by any standards but nevertheless it was superb piece of organisation to make it all work to time, especially in the summer period. Somebody, somewhere did not see the whole thing as a viable entity and with the stock requiring renewal and the whole system being non-standard from the sub station to the catenary, it was no wonder that the electric railway got the chop. *BLP 6282.*

A busy scene at Promenade station in July 1964 with Holbeck 'Jubilee' No.45573 NEWFOUNDLAND departing from platform No.2 with the 9.33 a.m. train to Leeds (City). An electric unit, lead by Driving Trailer Open Second M29022M, graces platform No.3 and an Ivatt Cl.2 tank is working the local service to Lancaster (Castle). Note that only platforms 1 and 2 have overhead cover in the shape of a canopy and that the electric services are confined to platforms 3 and 4. It appears that these platforms were never covered, at least not in the thirty years up to 1963. *BLP 6843.*

A welcome visitor to Morecambe in July 1964 was Kingmoor 'Clan' No.72007 CLAN MACKINTOSH, complete with nameplates for now. Within a couple of weeks No.72007 was to lose its plates but it is not known if Kingmoor painted replicas on the smoke deflectors as was the case with many of the Britannias in their care. Here, the Pacific had charge of a Carlisle bound parcels train and is just negotiating the pointwork between the goods yard and Promenade station throat. This engine was no stranger to the area during the summer of 1964 as it was used on the RCTS Ribble—Lune rail tour on the previous 23rd May when most of the lines in the Morecambe—Lancaster area due for closure were traversed by the Clan and its six-coach load. For that working it was presented in a somewhat cleaner condition - but beggars can't be choosers. The penultimate operational Clan, No.7 was condemned on 4th December 1965 and was towed away from Kingmoor to a scrapyard in Airdrie on Thursday 24th March 1966. *BLP 6837.*

July 1964. With all passenger traffic now diverted to Promenade station, this 2.25 p.m. departure for Crewe clears the junction with the closed Euston Road station as it heads along the former L&NW line. Immediately ahead of Newton Heath based 'Jubilee' No.45592 INDORE, is the one mile straight, and virtually level, run towards Bare Lane and then onto the junction which will put it eventually onto the WCML. The locomotive is on borrowed time (it certainly appears so) and by the end of the summer working will be condemned. By Christmas it will be in the hands of the Central Wagon Co. at Wigan. *BLP 6912.*

Seen from the bridge carrying the A5105 road over the WCML, Newton Heath based BR Standard 9F No.92077 brings a train of vans off the Morecambe line in July 1964. The rear of the train is still snaking off the curve where it runs alongside the main line. The latter can be seen veering off to the left towards Morecambe South junction. This is Lancashire countryside, something we have not seen too much of during our excursion from Warrington but for those travelling norhwards, like us, the vista started to open up. Shortly the wide expanse of Morecambe bay will spring into view on our left. Caravans, camping coaches and beaches suddenly appear because this part of the west coast is where one could indulge in a gentler holiday away from the bright lights, noise, crowds and attractions of the big resorts. *BLP 6887.* 59

The view from the north side of the same bridge reveals, two ex LMS 3F 'Jinties' Nos.47599 and 47317 getting to grips with a tank train in July 1964. They had brought the tanks from Carnforth and after crossing the junction just after Hest bank, were now en route to Morecambe. The train is travelling along the single track Morecambe line which ran parallel with the WCML for some distance before branching off towards Bare. Both the 0-6-0Ts were allocated to Green Ayre shed at this time and the day out to Carnforth, especially at this time of year was a decent working for the crews. The freight trip workings from Heysham and Morecambe to Carnforth were a regular job for the Lancaster tanks (as we have seen earlier). Note the target board with its crudely painted No.83. *BLP 6880.*

1964 saw the final summer for the 'Duchesses' and in July of that fateful year, No.46241 CITY OF EDINBURGH was undertaking one of its last workings before withdrawal on Saturday 5th September. The Crewe North based engine had spent the previous two winters in store but there would be no reprieve this time and once the summer timetable was finished so was No.41. The train is 1M32, the Glasgow (Central)—Morecambe (Promenade) holiday train which is taking the line to Morecambe in its stride. Turning the engine at Morecambe would not be a problem as the triangle of the Heysham lines was utilised to that affect. A year previously the sight of a 'Duchess' on this line was commonplace during the winter months because this route was used as a diversion to by-pass the Carlisle bridge rebuilding over the Lune. On arrival at Morecambe (Promenade), the main line trains and their motive power were hauled backwards along the Lancaster line to Green Ayre and once there they could resume their southbound journey using the Castle line to gain the WCML once again. *BLP 6903.* 61

Approaching Hest Bank from the south in July 1963, Carlisle Upperby based 'Royal Scot' No.46132 THE KING'S REGIMENT, LIVERPOOL has charge of a Down fitted freight. The relegation has really set in for these one time express passenger engines and this one has about six months work to do before withdrawal. At the end of the summer timetable the 'Scot' transferred to Kingmoor and although its mileage during its five months there was nothing compared with previous periods of time, it did manage to clock up its second million, albeit on jobs like this. Built in Scotland at NBL in 1927, it was dismantled there too at a scrapyard in Troon during 1965. Our photographer is stood at the end of the former goods yard where the camping coaches were berthed. Just beyond the footbridge in the distance was the A5105 road which crossed the railway on the skew bridge featured in some of the earlier illustrations. *BLP 6268.*

A lonely trainspotter, complete with regulation duffel bag, observes 'Duchess' No.46238 CITY OF CARLISLE running through Hest Bank station with a northbound parcels train in July 1963. Once again rain brings the sheen onto most surfaces although the Pacific has had some cleaning carried out at Crewe North shed before this duty. Hest Bank was one of the many BR locations where camping coaches became fixed features in the nearby sidings for many years; the sea would usually be but a stones throw away too. Those who 'billeted' in them apparently enjoyed themselves even though the majority had no inclination to observe trains or note the numbers of passing engines. What a pity that such facilities do not exist today for those who would want to observe the comings and goings of the railway traffic in comfort. Just think back to the BR's steam era, say circa 1956 - two weeks in one of those old coaches, rain or shine, feet up, tea or other beverage in hand, watching the trains come and go! *BLP 6257.*

This time we look north from Hest Bank station footbridge. Crewe North 'Jubilee' No.45553 CANADA pulls away with a Manchester (Victoria)—Barrow train in July 1963. Note the headboard adorning the fairly new Mk.1 coach, M35208, which appears to have an exclusively all-female clientele; perhaps the males have 'bagged' all the forward facing seats for a better view; in doing so they are hidden from us. Discernible in the distance, through the summer drizzle, are the Hest Bank water troughs which were still operational at this time but alas not for much longer. Their upkeep and maintenance would have been one headache which BR would have welcomed to see the back of as steam traction came to the end of its reign. *BLP 6258.*

Having just stopped to have a word with the signalman, much to the chagrin of waiting motorist no doubt, 'Britannia' No.70000 BRITANNIA pulls away over the level crossing at Hest Bank in July 1964 with his instructions - whatever they might have been. The train is 1M32 again but with a different type of Pacific in charge. No.70000 had not long been on the strength of Crewe North's allocation after transfer from the Eastern Region during the previous June. Note that the smoke deflectors now have the circular hand holds fitted, a recent ER modification from the original hand rails. By now the class was sporting three different types of hand holds - oblong, circular and rails. By December 1964 most of the Eastern Region 'Brits' would have spent some time in storage but during that month they were gradually being released to the Midland Region to another stint of work. Many arrived 'dead' at Kingmoor and had to be revived prior to going back into traffic - the Eastern had gone diesel! *BLP 6823.*

65

Long before the gradual run-down of steam motive power, classes not normally associated with certain traffics would do their bit when the need arose. Here at Hest Bank on a warm summer evening in August 1957, Crewe North 'Jubilee' No.45678 (how about that for a number sequence!) DE ROBECK, approaches the north end of the station with an Up goods train. *BLP 489*.

Taking photographs of the passing trains whilst standing next to water troughs could be a risky business, certainly a wet one, but Don Beecroft was in luck on this July Saturday in 1963 when Crewe North 'Royal Scot' No.46155 THE LANCER had charge of a Saturdays Only Glasgow (St Enoch)—Morecambe (Promenade) express at Hest Bank. The 4-6-0 must have picked up enough water at Dillicar troughs and with Morecambe being so close the crew must have deemed it not to be worth the bother of lowering the scoop. Once beyond Hest Bank and the overbridge the train will slow considerably for the change of route onto the triangle at Bare, or Torrisholme, which was another title given to the single line curve. THE LANCER was one of the 1930 Derby built 'Scots' which managed to work for the whole of its life on the WCML and its branches. *BLP 6270.*

Right! We will sit in this field with our deck chairs and face them towards the sun and perhaps get a nice tan. At the same time we can observe the trains and take some pictures for the holiday album. Seems a good idea for the spotters in the family but the rest of them might get restless after a while - who knows - lets give it a try whilst the sun is out. All that sand just gets between your toes anyway, not to mention other more sensitive places. We are in a field next to the WCML somewhere near Hest Bank in July 1963. The position of the sun indicates mid afternoon as does the arrival of the Down LAKES EXPRESS which has just breezed by with 'Duchess' No.46254 CITY OF STOKE ON TRENT in charge. Now, how do you expect to get a tan with your shirts on? *BLP 6274.*

The Up CALEDONIAN, with immaculate 'Duchess' No.46242 CITY OF GLASGOW at the helm, passes a Down goods near Bolton-le-Sands on a beautiful August morning in 1957. Virtually level and dead straight, this section of the WCML became something of a racetrack for the Anglo-Scottish expresses during the reign of steam. *BLP 495*.

Being the chief depot in the District, Carnforth engine shed looked after the basic needs of the other sheds within that same district. One of the numerous jobs of the 'head shed' in early BR days was to store serviceable locomotives which would otherwise be in the way at their home sheds. Space was usually at a premium at most depots though Carnforth appeared to have a bit more siding space than most. Tucked away in a siding on the west side of the shed yard on 28th August 1955 were a number of ancient pre-Grouping engines which were stored in a serviceable condition. Amongst them were these two former L&NWR Webb '18in Goods' 0-6-0s, Nos.58409 and 58412. Both engines were allocated to Penrith at this time and had been for a number of years but they were getting a bit long in the tooth at 55 years of age. In the summer of 1935, for instance, the 0-6-0s had been together at Aston shed in Birmingham and from there they appeared to have stayed together since, as here. The tenders of both locomotives carry the wooden protection frame which was used when engaged on snow plough duties. No doubt their time at Penrith shed saw them used for that kind of work on the line through Keswick to Cockermouth and perhaps eastwards towards Appleby. However, by December 1955 they would be inside the confines of Crewe works, condemned to the scrap heap and history. *K.R.Pirt 98F.4.*

At the Grouping Carnforth was blessed with three separate engine sheds. The Furness Railway had a reasonable establishment on the site of what was to become the new LMS shed built during WW2 and brought into use in 1944. The London & North Western Railway had a six road shed a little to the south of the FR shed and on the same side of the WCML. The Midland Railway had the usual square roundhouse shed which was located on the line to Wennington, to the north of and slightly east of the town. All three sheds were operational until 1944 although the exFR shed was demolished some time before, to make way for its LMS successor, so its locomotives used the L&NWR facilities when necessary. The wartime depot was provided with mechanical servicing apparatus in the shape of a coaling plant and ash plant, both in picture here, and a six road through shed which is out of frame to the left. In August 1955 one of the remnants of the Furness company was stored on the western siding along with the exLNW 0-6-0s mentioned previously. This is Pettigrew 3F 0-6-0 No.52509 of Workington shed, one of five still existing from the nineteen strong class which entered the LMS at Grouping. Unlike the LNW engines, this 0-6-0 would survive a little longer and it would be December 1956 when it made its final journey to Horwich and oblivion. K.R.Pirt 98F.3.

We have not had many BR Standards in this album so lets finish off with Cl.5 No.73142 bringing a Barrow—Morecambe train through Carnforth in July 1964. We are now in the former Furness Railway section of the station which, as can be seen, was rather modern (1960s point of view) yet somewhat austere and cold. Across the other platform and then over the WCML tracks, we can see part of the original station which offered a more homely feel, albeit grimy - a bit like the Standard. Besides being a bastion of steam power when it all ended, then as a centre for preserved steam, Carnforth's only other claim to fame was the fact that a certain feature film was enacted there, right on the station, perhaps in the refreshment rooms on the Up platform. It might not be possible to pick out the rain on this picture but yes it was falling, but what do you expect on the west coast of Lancashire in summer? *BLP 6846.*